Cambridge Discovery Readers

Level 4

Series editor: Nicholas Tims

Bullring Kid and Country Cowboy

Louise Clover

CAMBRIDGE
UNIVERSITY PRESS

Shaftesbury Road, Cambridge CB2 8EA, United Kingdom

One Liberty Plaza, 20th Floor, New York, NY 10006, USA

477 Williamstown Road, Port Melbourne, VIC 3207, Australia

314–321, 3rd Floor, Plot 3, Splendor Forum, Jasola District Centre,
New Delhi – 110025, India

103 Penang Road, #05-06/07, Visioncrest Commercial, Singapore 238467

Cambridge University Press & Assessment is a department of the University of Cambridge.

We share the University's mission to contribute to society through the pursuit of
education, learning and research at the highest international levels of excellence.

www.cambridge.org

This American English edition is based on *Bullring Kid and Country Cowboy*,
ISBN 978-84-832-3495-2 first published by Cambridge University Press in 2009.

First published 2009
American English edition 2010

20 19 18 17 16 15 14 13 12 11 10 9

Printed in Great Britain by CPI Group (UK) Ltd, Croydon CR0 4YY

ISBN 978-0-521-14891-7 Paperback American English edition

Illustrations by Albert Asensio

Edited by Carol Giscombe

Audio recording by hyphen

Exercises by Peter McDonnell

Contents

People in the story

Fizza McIntyre: a fifteen-year-old girl from Birmingham, England

Fletcher McIntyre: a fifteen-year-old boy from the small island of Sark; he was born and raised in the U.S.

Imran McIntyre: Fizza's dad

Rubel McIntyre: Fizza's mom

Richard McIntyre: Fletcher's dad

Babs: Fizza's best friend

Billy Adams: one of the most popular boys in Fizza's school

Robert Scully: a rich businessman

BEFORE YOU READ

1 Look at the cover and the pictures in the first two chapters. Answer the question.

Do you think that Fizza is the Country Cowboy?

Chapter 1

The Judo Kid

"Oof!"

For the fifth time, Fizza's dad threw her over his back and onto the grass.

"Ow! I wasn't ready, Dad!" she screamed.

"That's no excuse, Fizza! You have to always be ready!" replied her father. "You might be a girl – but it doesn't stop you from being as brave as a man."

Fizza picked herself up from the ground and faced her judo teacher. Imran McIntyre was half-Scottish, half-Pakistani, and one hundred percent crazy. They had been practicing judo for over an hour in the late afternoon sunshine and she was getting really tired now. However, she still managed to take her dad by surprise. Although she was feeling weak, she suddenly ran at him and threw him to the ground.

"Fizza! Leave your poor father alone!" called her mother from the house. "Anyway, it's time for tea."

"Thanks, Rubel! You saved me from the crazy judo kid!" said Imran.

He got up and took Fizza's hand and, laughing together, they went into the house.

It was Thursday, so Fizza knew what her mom had made for tea. Every week it was the same, because it was her dad's favorite meal.

"Oh no, I hate fish curry!" thought Fizza as she sat down at the table.

The fish curry was always so hot it set her mouth on fire – and she *hated* fish. However, to keep her mom and dad happy, she ate her food without complaining.

"So are you looking forward to our holiday[1], Fizza?" asked her dad.

"No—," thought Fizza.

"Yes, she is!" interrupted her mom. "Aren't you, darling?"

Fizza smiled falsely through a horrible mouthful of curry.

"I can't wait! I love the Channel Islands, but this will be the first time I've been to Sark," said Fizza's dad as he greedily[2] took another big spoonful of food from the bowl. "It's the smallest of the islands, isn't it?"

"Yes, and no cars are allowed there, so it's going to be quiet! Fresh air and no pollution[3]!" said her mom.

"How wonderful!" said Imran.

"How boring!" thought Fizza.

Fizza's mom, Rubel, worked for Birmingham Council[4] in the Environmental Office. It was her job to make Birmingham cleaner and "greener," but it was a difficult job with so many cars and factories in the city. There was also too much garbage. So a vacation on an island with no cars was her idea of a perfect vacation. However, it was not Fizza's idea of a perfect vacation. She loved the city. She loved Birmingham! It was busy! It was loud! It was home!

"Right!" said Imran, as he finished his meal. "Come on, Fizza – let's practice some more judo."

"But I wanted to go on the computer," said Fizza.

"Felicity," said her mom, "you're always on that computer."

It was true. Fizza loved her computer. She spent hours working on different programs and she was the best in her class in information technology. It was the one school subject that she knew she was good at.

"But I want to talk to my friends," she replied.

"Can't you use the phone?" said her mom. "Or better still, go and visit them – like I did when I was a girl?"

"And you won't get any better at judo unless you practice!" said her dad.

Fizza sighed[5] deeply. It was always the same thing. Her mom thought she used her computer too much and her dad thought that she should be an Olympic judo champion.

Fizza's dad thought that judo was the most important thing in the world. When he wasn't practicing it, he was talking about it. He had taken up judo as a small boy and eventually he had become National Champion of Scotland. However, Fizza did not love it as much as her dad.

"Actually Fizza, I think you're really making progress now," he said. "You'll be a champion yet! But I've told you before, you should join a judo club!"

Once again Fizza sighed. She didn't mind practicing in the yard, but she didn't want to join a judo club because judo wasn't "cool." Her best friend Babs didn't do judo and nor did any of the other "cool" girls.

"Dad! Are you crazy?" she said.

"I'm sorry?" said her father.

"You teach me everything. What else can a club teach me?" said Fizza.

Imran laughed at this sweet talk and Fizza jumped up from the table.

"Come on, old man. Let's have a race to the yard – and I promise I'll be gentle with you!"

*   *   *

At about six thirty, the doorbell rang.

"Fizza!" her mom called up the stairs. "Babs is here!"

Fizza ran down the stairs. Her friend was waiting for her in the hallway.

"Hi, Babs!" she said.

"Fizza! I had to come and tell you something!" said Babs, who was obviously very excited.

"Oh? What is it?"

"I've just been to the shops[6] and guess who was on the bus!" she said.

"The Queen?"

"What? No, don't be stupid. Billy Adams!"

"Who?"

"Fizza! You know! He's that seriously good-looking guy at school!"

Babs wanted to go out with Billy, but so did all the girls in their grade. He was very popular with girls.

"And?" said Fizza.

"And what?" replied Babs.

"Well, what happened?"

"Well, he looked at me. Well, I *think* he looked at me – he looked near me because he sat in front of me."

"And he had the whole of the bus to choose from?"

"Yeah!"

Fizza didn't like to say it was probably just luck that Billy had sat in front of her.

"Wow!" she replied.

"I know!" said Babs.

Fizza smiled. She had been good friends with Babs since they had joined the school at the age of eleven. For four years they had done everything together: laughed, played games, shared secrets, and laughed some more. However, recently Fizza felt that something had changed, because something new had arrived in Babs's life. In fact two things had arrived: boys and fashion. Babs had stopped wearing school uniform and she had started dressing in the same way as the scary "cool" girls. And although Fizza secretly wanted to be "cool," she *did* still wear school uniform and outside of school she just wore jeans, T-shirts, and sneakers. She wasn't really interested in wearing stupid clothes or makeup – especially for boys.

Fizza's mom said that she was pretty but then, she thought, her mom would say that, wouldn't she? She had thick, black hair which she always wore tied back, brown eyes, a button nose, and a mouth which she thought made her look like a frog. It didn't help that she was small and thin for a fifteen-year-old, because it made her look younger than all the other girls.

Fizza knew she and Babs could still be friends and they could still share secrets. But the secrets were different now. They weren't about sweet baby animals or a house with a ghost at the end of the street. They were about boys like Billy.

"Well," said Fizza. "He'll be at school tomorrow!"

"Ooh! I know! I know!" said Babs. "I can't wait! I'm going to make myself talk to him! And Fizza, you're going to help me!"

Chapter 2

Fizza is cool for ten minutes

The next day was the last day of the school term and there were no proper classes. No one was going to do any work that day. Hundreds of children moved from class to class, talking excitedly about their summer vacations. Fizza sat in the computer classroom and listened. She heard about trips to Disneyland, summer camps in the U.S., and vacations in Spain, Italy, and Portugal. Babs was telling a group of the scary "cool" girls in their class about her sailing vacation with her cousins in Greece. Fizza pretended to be busy working on the computer so she didn't have to tell anyone about her vacation on the very quiet, pollution-free island of Sark.

Suddenly four boys ran into the classroom, laughing and shouting. Fizza noticed that one of them was Billy Adams, the "seriously good-looking guy" that Babs had seen on the bus the evening before. Fizza smiled to herself when she saw Babs cover her face with her hands in embarrassment. The group of "cool" girls whispered to one another in excitement at the boys' arrival. These boys didn't care about school; they just wanted to have a laugh. They were always in trouble with the teachers, which made them even more attractive to girls. Fizza hid shyly behind her computer.

"Who's good at computers in here?" asked Billy.

The girls looked at one another. They all knew how to use chatrooms but not much else.

"Why?" asked one of them.

"I need help with some pictures."

"I know who can help you, Billy!" someone said in a voice that was a bit too high and a bit too loud.

Fizza looked out from behind her computer to see who had spoken; she was surprised to see it was a very red-faced Babs. And when Billy Adams turned to look at her, she turned from red to purple! Fizza thought her poor friend was about to explode with embarrassment.

"Yeah?" he said.

"Fizza."

"Who?" said Billy.

Babs pointed at Fizza.

"That's Fizza. She's good at computers."

Everyone looked at Fizza. She wanted to hide under her desk.

"Oh, great. Thanks," said Billy and walked over to where Fizza was sitting.

"Hi, Fizza," he said.

"Hi," she managed to whisper.

"Could you do something with this?" said Billy as he sat down beside her and gave her a CD. She stared at it.

"It's pictures of the teachers," he said, smiling. "I want to give them an end-of-term 'present'."

Fizza put the CD into the computer. After a minute pictures of all their teachers appeared.

"Now, Fizza," said Billy, moving closer to her.

He was so close she could feel his breath on her cheek and it smelled of chewing gum. She had to admit to herself that he *was* good-looking: he had clear blue eyes and short, fair hair, and a gentle smile. However, she kept staring at the computer screen; she was way too shy to look at him directly.

"Do you think you could put *his* head on *her* body?" Billy continued.

He pointed at a picture of Mr. Roberts, their science teacher, who wore glasses and had hardly any hair. Then he pointed at Miss Simmons, the English teacher, who was small and fat and wore a bright pink dress. Fizza smiled. She thought it was a really funny idea.

"Of course I can," she said and she began to work.

Once she had finished with Mr. Roberts and Miss Simmons, she moved on to Miss Brown, the very slim and pretty history teacher. Miss Brown received the principal's head and the hairy legs of the gym teacher. By the time she had finished with Mr. Jones, the poor math teacher, he was wearing a short skirt and had a long, gray beard.

"Amazing!" said Billy as everyone crowded around the computer screen.

He then turned to Fizza, looked directly at her and smiled.

"Thanks, Fizza, you're really cool," he said.

Then the boys left the classroom and the scary girls stared at Fizza. They obviously couldn't believe that dull Fizza McIntyre had been given so much attention by the wonderful Billy Adams.

"Wow! I can't believe it!" whispered Babs, as she sat down beside Fizza.

Fizza smiled back at her; she couldn't believe it either. One of the coolest boys in the school had called her cool!

"Fizza! Listen! Do you think Billy likes me?" said Babs. "He *did* speak to me!"

"I'm sure he likes you," said Fizza. "Who wouldn't?"

And smiling to herself, she turned back to the computer screen.

* * *

It was the second week of the school vacation and Fizza was at the stores with her mom. They were in the Bullring Shopping Centre in Birmingham.

She was feeling a bit strange because she had just had her hair cut. Her mom and the hairdresser had both agreed that her new haircut looked fantastic.

"But then," Fizza thought, "they would say that, wouldn't they?"

She didn't really care what they thought, because secretly she had had her hair cut for someone else. Fizza McIntyre didn't want to admit it to anyone, but something had changed inside her. Every day since the end of term, she had looked at herself in her bedroom mirror.

"He called me cool," she told the mirror. "He called me cool."

The truth was she wanted to look "cool" not for herself – but for Billy Adams.

The shopping center was full of bored teenagers wasting time on their school vacations. As she followed her mom out of a shoe store, she turned a corner and walked straight into a group of boys from school. In the middle of them was Billy Adams!

Fizza could feel her face getting hot. She wanted to run and hide. She wanted to be somewhere else, anywhere but right there at that moment in the Bullring Shopping Centre. Then she remembered what her dad told her every time they practiced judo.

"Fizza, you might be a girl," he said, "but it doesn't stop you from being as brave as a man."

So she made herself be brave. She looked straight at Billy and gave him a great big smile.

"Hi, Billy," she said.

Billy looked at her … and then he looked away.

"Who's that?" Fizza heard one of his friends say to him.

"I don't know," replied Billy.

Fizza felt terrible. Billy didn't want to know her! She could feel hot tears in her eyes and she wanted to run away, but she couldn't – she had to walk, she had to be "cool."

"Me? Cool?" she thought. "Forget it."

For the first time, she was really glad[7] that she was going away to the island of Sark and she followed her mother out of the shopping center as quickly as she could.

However, Fizza didn't know that Billy Adams was watching her walk away. He hadn't recognized her with her new haircut – but he *had* thought that she was a very pretty girl.

ACTIVITIES

. . . .

1 Check your answers to *Before you read* on page 4.

2 Complete the summary of Chapters 1 and 2 with the words in the box.

Felicity	Greece	Babs (x2)	boys	Billy
Rubel	Imran	judo	Birmingham	

Fizza, whose real name is [1] *Felicity* , lives with her parents in a big, busy city in the middle of England named [2]............... . Her mom, [3]..............., works for the local council. Her dad, [4]..............., loves two things in life — fish curry, which Fizza hates, and his favorite sport, [5]..............., which he teaches Fizza in the yard. Fizza, however, prefers spending time working on her computer. It's her best subject in school, but her mom thinks she spends too much time on it. Fizza's best friend, [6]..............., is very different. She's more interested in fashion and boys, especially [7]............... Adams, who goes to the same school. On the last day of school, everyone is talking about the exciting places they are going to in the summer. [8]..............., for example, is going sailing in [9]............... . Fizza, however, is too embarrassed to tell everyone that she is only going to [10]..............., a quiet island with no cars.

3 Are the sentences true (*T*) or false (*F*)?
1 Fizza is looking forward to her vacation. ☐ *F*
2 Fizza's dad doesn't think she's good at judo. ☐
3 Babs and Fizz don't wear the same kind of clothes. ☐
4 The other girls in school look older than Fizza. ☐
5 Fizza was working when Billy came into the classroom. ☐
6 Fizza had her hair cut for Billy. ☐
7 Billy was interested in Fizza when he saw her at the shopping center. ☐

4 Match the two parts of the sentences.
1 Fizza doesn't want to join a judo club because ☐ *d*
2 Fizza wants to be cool although ☐
3 Babs is very embarrassed when ☐
4 Fizza is surprised when ☐

a she doesn't admit it to anyone.
b Billy speaks to her and the other girls.
c Billy says she is cool.
d it's not cool.

5 Answer the questions.
1 Why is Sark a good place for Rubel to go on vacation?

....

2 Why are the other girls surprised that Billy spoke to Fizza?

....

LOOKING FORWARD

6 Check (✓) what you think happens in the next four chapters.
1 Billy becomes Fizza's boyfriend. ☐
2 Billy becomes Babs's boyfriend. ☐
3 Fizza has a good time on vacation. ☐

Chapter 3

The island that time forgot

Fizza looked out across the field from the white cottage[8] that she was sharing with her mom and dad. She looked down the rocky coast. Then she looked at the boats parked in a neat line in the little harbor down below. The boat that they had arrived on earlier in the day was just beginning its return trip to the island of Guernsey and she watched it disappear across the deep blue sea, shining in the afternoon sunshine. To her left, coming up the hill, she could see a large brown horse pulling a carriage[9] full of tourists, and in the distance she saw a man driving a tractor across a field. Fizza McIntyre could see lots of things, but she couldn't hear anything. The island of Sark was quiet – deadly quiet. It was so quiet it made Fizza feel uncomfortable. However, her mom was feeling very comfortable!

"Isn't this exciting, Fizza!" said Rubel McIntyre, coming out of the cottage door, drying her hands on a towel. "You can just smell the peace, can't you?"

Fizza pretended to yawn. "Exciting" was the last word she would use to describe this place. She already knew that this vacation was going to be the most boring one ever.

She kicked a rock, which unfortunately hit her mom's foot.

"Ow! Look out! Why are you so angry, young lady?"

"Sorry. I'm just tired. Sorry."

Fizza was in a bad mood, but she was tired, too. They had started their trip from Birmingham at six o'clock that

morning. They had driven for four hours to catch the boat to Guernsey. Then they had taken a smaller boat to Sark, where they had been met by a horse and carriage! Eventually they had arrived at a cottage which didn't even have a TV – and there was certainly no Internet. Fizza knew that this vacation was going to be a complete failure! She was even looking forward to going back to school!

However, there had been one thing that had made Fizza smile a little bit that day.

As their boat arrived that morning, all the passengers had been met by a line of horses and carriages – the island's taxi service. Their "taxi" was from "The Richard McIntyre Horse and Carriage Company" and their driver was a tall man in his forties, with curly brown hair and a happy suntanned face.

"Hi! My name is Richard McIntyre," he had said.

As soon as he had spoken, Fizza had realized he was American.

"And I'm Imran McIntyre!" Fizza's dad had laughed. "What are the chances of that!"

"We've come all this way only to meet someone with exactly the same last name!" her mom had said.

And everyone had laughed, including Fizza, as Richard McIntyre put their luggage onto the carriage and drove them up the hill.

"Are you from Sark?" Fizza had asked him, shyly.

Richard McIntyre laughed.

"You noticed! No, I'm from the Rocky Mountains in Colorado. We came to live here three years ago. And where are you from?" he had asked.

"Ah, Birmingham – a bit different from Sark, I imagine."

"Yes. It's big! It's noisy!" her mom had answered.

"It's great!" Fizza had thought.

"And what about pollution?" asked Richard. "On Sark we have no cars, so we have almost no pollution!"

"Oh yes," her mom had said, "I'm sorry to say we have a lot of pollution in Birmingham."

"We also have a lot of nice things to do in Birmingham," Fizza had thought, staring out of the back of the carriage and wondering what Billy Adams was doing at that minute. He wasn't on some smelly horse carriage – she was sure of that.

"Oh, you'll love Sark! They call it the island that time forgot," Richard had said.

"I wish I could forget about it," Fizza had thought.

*   *   *

And so it was that Fizza found herself on "the island that time forgot" with absolutely nothing to do. Her mom's voice brought her out of her dream and back to the present moment.

"Why don't you go and explore, Fizza?" said her mom. "By the time you get back, I'll have supper ready. Oh! And get your dad a newspaper, please."

Fizza went down the hill toward the little village at the bottom. In five minutes she had discovered two bicycle rental stores, three stores that sold jewelry and jugs, and a tiny post office that was also a supermarket. Fizza went up to the counter.

"Do you sell newspapers?" she asked a small gray-haired lady.

"Sorry," she said, "they didn't arrive from Guernsey today. Try tomorrow."

"What is this place?" thought Fizza. "There aren't even any newspapers!"

She thanked the lady and left the store. As she began the climb back up the hill, she passed a group of girls of about her age. They were chewing gum and wearing short skirts. They looked just like the "cool" girls from school, which made Fizza smile.

"Some things never change," she thought, "wherever you go."

And she began to run back toward the cottage.

Later, after supper, Fizza and her dad practiced judo in the field behind the cottage. For over an hour they threw one another onto the grass until Imran admitted defeat and went inside to play a game of cards with Rubel.

As the sun began to drop down from the sky like a great big orange, Fizza continued to practice her judo moves. Eventually she got tired and stopped. She looked out at the dark gray sea and breathed in deeply. And for the first time since she had arrived on Sark, she found herself listening. She could hear the birds singing good night to each other, and the sound of sheep bells and a boat in the distance. Then, lifting her nose into the air, she breathed in deeply and she found that the evening air of Sark smelled sweet. It was completely different from the heavy city smell of her much-loved Birmingham. Such beauty suddenly made Fizza McIntyre feel alive and she decided to show the island how good she felt.

"Good night, Sark!" she shouted as she jumped high in the air and then fell on the grass.

Laughing at herself for being silly, she picked herself up and turned to go indoors, but immediately she came to a stop.

Sitting in a tree beside the cottage was a red-haired boy who looked about the same age as her. For a minute they stared at one another until her attention was taken by a small brown rabbit that ran past her. She took her eyes away from the boy for just a few seconds and during this time he completely disappeared.

Chapter 4

Fizza meets Fletcher

The next morning Fizza was woken up by her mother.

"Come on, you lazy girl! Get up! Richard's outside – he's going to take us on a tour of the island!"

Fizza opened one eye and looked at her watch. It said seven o'clock. "Hey! I'm on holiday!" she said as she put her pillow over her head.

"Come on! Richard says it's the best time of day to see the island – before it gets too crowded."

"Crowded? Here?" thought Fizza. "That doesn't seem likely."

Eventually, when she had washed, brushed her teeth and quickly eaten some breakfast, she stepped outside. Her mom, dad, and Richard McIntyre and his horse and carriage were waiting for her.

"Good morning, young lady!" he said cheerfully.

"Is it?" asked Fizza, yawning.

"Of course it is!" Richard laughed. "The sun's out! So are you ready?"

"Yeah, I'm ready …" said Fizza.

She wondered if Richard McIntyre was always this happy. Still sleepy, she climbed up on the carriage and they began their trip across the island.

For the next few hours the carriage moved slowly past trees, fields, a few houses, and tractors. It also moved past other carriages carrying tourists. They saw small beaches, rocks on the coast and black holes, which Richard said were caves. They went from Derrible Bay to Dixcart Bay, and then past a large golden beach at La Grand Grève. The adults talked about the countryside and about towns, and Rubel McIntyre told Richard about her job as an environmental officer.

"I think that Birmingham could learn something from Sark," she said.

"Well, why don't you start by getting rid of all the cars and telling everyone to buy a horse?" said Richard.

And they all laughed except for Fizza, who was beginning to feel sick at the back of the carriage.

They continued their trip.

"If you don't care, I'd like to go to the Venus Pool. It's a beautiful little beach where my son likes fishing. Hopefully we'll see him."

As they arrived at a small beach, they saw a tall boy wearing jeans, a white T-shirt, a blue baseball cap, and no shoes. He was sitting on a rock beside a pile of large silver fish.

"Hey, Fletcher!" called Richard. "Any luck?"

"Yes! I caught six big ones!"

"Great! Do you want a ride?"

Without another word, the boy climbed down off the rock, picked up his fish, and ran over to the carriage.

"This is my son, Fletcher," said Richard. "And this is Imran, Rubel … and, I'm sorry Rubel – I don't know your daughter's name!" he said to Fizza's mom.

"Fizza," said her mom, "Fizza McIntyre."

"Do you hear that, Fletcher? This young lady is a McIntyre!"

"So?" said Fletcher rudely.

"Fletcher and Fizza! Two F. McIntyres!" laughed Richard. "You two should get along really well."

All the adults laughed as, without smiling, the boy sat down beside her. Fizza could feel her face burning with embarrassment. The boy kept his face hidden under his cap and held the fish in his arms. They made Fizza feel even sicker.

24

She even hated the smell of fish. Then she noticed that he didn't have a fishing rod or even a net.

"Where's your fishing rod?" she asked.

"I don't have one," he said, without looking at her.

"Oh? So how did you catch them?" she asked.

Fletcher just held his dirty hands up in front of her and then turned his back on her.

"He caught those fish with his hands? I don't think so!" thought Fizza, taking an immediate dislike to this rude boy. And they didn't speak again for the rest of the trip.

* * *

Later, after supper, Fizza was practicing her judo outside the cottage when she noticed a dark shape coming down the hill. As it got closer, she realized it was a black and white horse that was being ridden very quickly. She jumped out of the way to let it pass. Although the animal was so close she could hear its heavy breath, she couldn't see who the rider was because their face was covered by a green scarf.

Horses scared Fizza – especially when they were going that fast.

"Stupid fool," she said as she watched the dangerous rider disappear down the hill.

The next evening, after a pleasant day on the beach, Fizza was practicing her judo when she saw the black and white horse again. This time its rider had stopped it at the top of the field and they appeared to be looking down at the cottage. They remained like this for a few seconds before riding away. Fizza was sure that it was the same horse and probably the same rider. But who was it?

On the third evening Fizza's mom and dad made plans for dinner.

"Fizza, we thought we'd go to the restaurant in the village tonight," said her dad. "Would you like that?"

Fizza had to think quickly. She didn't want to be away from the cottage. She didn't want to miss the mystery horse.

"Oh, thanks, but I'm feeling really tired this evening – I'd rather just have some soup and read my book."

"Oh, we'll all stay here then!" said her mom.

"No, no – you go, I'll be fine," replied Fizza quickly.

She said good-bye to her mom and dad, who promised to be home before it was dark, and went out into the field again to practice her judo moves. It was another beautiful evening, but after about an hour the sun began to set and Fizza began to feel tired. And this time there had been no sign of the black and white horse. She turned to go inside, but as she walked past the tree beside the cottage, one of the branches crashed down and somebody fell on top of her. Without thinking, she threw the person over her shoulder and onto the ground.

"Ow!"

It was a tall boy wearing jeans, a white T-shirt, no shoes, and a blue baseball cap, which fell off to show thick, red hair, and a pair of the angriest green eyes Fizza had ever seen. It was Fletcher, Richard McIntyre's son!

"You!" said Fizza. "Were you spying on me?"

"No!"

"Yes, you were! I saw you the other night, too!"

Fletcher changed the subject. "Anyway, you've broken my ankle!" he said, holding his leg.

"*I* broke your ankle? *You* were in the tree! You broke your own ankle!"

"Ow!" said Fletcher again.

Fizza suddenly felt a bit guilty for throwing him onto the ground.

"Do you think you can walk?" she asked a little more gently. Fletcher shook his head.

"Here, put your arm around me. I'll help you to get up."

With some difficulty, Fletcher stood up and Fizza helped him into the cottage where she sat him on a kitchen chair.

"Do you really think you've broken it?" she asked. "Can you move it?"

She didn't know why she asked him that, but it was what people said in movies.

"Yeah, a bit," said Fletcher.

"Well, should I ask your dad to come and get you?"

"If you want," he replied.

Fizza, annoyed by this boy's rudeness again, called his father on her cell. By the time Richard McIntyre arrived, so had Fizza's mom and dad.

"What have you been doing, Fletcher?" laughed Richard.

"Nothing," said Fletcher. "I fell out of a tree, that's all. It's feeling better now."

"Come on, let's get you home. Say thank you to Fizza," Fletcher's dad said.

"Thanks," said Fletcher quietly, as his dad helped him to leave the kitchen.

Through the window in the evening light, Fizza watched Richard McIntyre help Fletcher to get up onto a horse. There was no mistake. It was the black and white horse.

Chapter 5

The horses up the hill

The next morning Fizza was woken by a loud crash outside her bedroom window.

Rubbing her eyes, she looked at her watch. It said 12:15. How could she have slept for so long? Her thoughts were interrupted by more noise from outside.

"Oof!"

"Hup!"

"Oomph!"

It was the sound of two men fighting. Quickly she pulled back the curtain just in time to see her father throwing Richard McIntyre over his left shoulder.

"Ow!" screamed Richard. "My back!"

"You're still not landing correctly!" replied her dad. "Let's try again."

"Shouldn't we have a cup of coffee first, Imran?" asked Richard.

Fizza thought he sounded rather hopeful.

"No! Come on! You can do this!"

Fizza smiled to herself. Poor Richard! She knew how he had to be feeling. Once her dad found a new judo student, he didn't let them escape easily.

A few minutes later Fizza stepped out of the cottage and into the sunshine.

"Good morning, Fizza," said her dad. "Or should I say good afternoon?"

"Hi, Fizza," said Richard, smiling up at her from his position on the grass.

"This Sark air makes you sleep deeply, doesn't it?"

It was true, she never slept so deeply at home.

"Yeah," she said. "Where's Fletcher today? How's his ankle?"

"Oh, his ankle's fine! He's driving one of my carriages for me so I have the morning off—"

"And so I'm giving him some judo classes!" said her dad, putting out his hand to pull poor Richard back onto his feet.

"But I could tell him that you're hoping to see him!" continued Richard.

"Who?" said Fizza.

"Fletcher!"

"No, it's OK!" said Fizza quickly, but it was too late. Richard had already taken his cell phone from his pocket.

"Fletcher! Is everything OK?" he shouted into the phone.

As Richard listened to his son's answer, Fizza tried to stop herself from screaming and running down the hill. Why did all adults have to embarrass her all the time? She didn't want to see that rude boy!

"Guess what, Fletcher!" Richard continued. "I'm here with Fizza McIntyre at the cottage. Why don't you come over when you've finished?"

Poor Fizza thought she was going to explode with embarrassment, just like the time she saw Billy Adams in the Bullring Shopping Centre.

"And you have to both stay for lunch!" said her mom, coming out of the cottage carrying two mugs of coffee.

"Could this get any worse?" thought Fizza.

At lunch the three adults talked happily but Fizza and Fletcher, who were sitting side by side, sat quietly without looking at one another.

"Thank you, Rubel! That was a delicious fish curry!" said Richard as he put down his knife and fork.

"Thank you," said Fizza's mom. "It's Fizza's favorite, isn't it, darling?"

Fizza made such a horrible face that it made Fletcher laugh out loud.

"At least he finds some things funny," she thought.

"Thanks a lot for lunch," said Richard. "Now I wonder if I could—"

Before he could finish his sentence, Fizza's dad had jumped up from the table.

"Do some more judo?"

"Uh, thanks, Imran," said Richard, "but I have another suggestion. Would you like to come and visit a friend who lives on the other side of the island? She makes beautiful pots."

"How wonderful!" said Fizza's mom.

"I'd rather do some more judo," said her dad.

"Imran!" said Rubel angrily. "We'd love to, thank you Richard. What about you, Fizza?"

Fizza wanted to say that she would rather eat fish curry than go and visit someone who makes pots, but, being a polite girl, she kept quiet.

"Maybe Fizza would like to stay behind with Fletcher?" said Richard.

Fizza could feel her face turning red again.

"Fletcher," he said, "why don't you introduce Fizza to our horses?"

Fizza thought it would also be a bit rude if she said she didn't like horses.

"If she wants," said Fletcher, without looking at her.

* * *

The two fifteen-year-olds watched as Richard McIntyre drove Rubel and Imran McIntyre in his horse and carriage down the coast road into the distance. Eventually the carriage disappeared from view, but they remained standing in silence. Fizza was beginning to wonder if they were going to stay like that all afternoon.

"So do you want to see the horses or not?" said Fletcher suddenly.

Fizza turned to face him and for the first time they looked at one another properly.

She could see a boy who had wide green eyes and little brown freckles on his nose, and he could see a girl with warm, kind eyes, and thick, black hair that curled around her pretty face. At exactly the same moment, they smiled at one another.

"Yes, that would be great," replied Fizza.

"Come on, we keep all the horses in the stables just up the hill. Are you OK walking?"

"Of course I am!" replied Fizza.

"Oh yeah, I forgot. You are good at sports – for a girl."

"Thanks. And you're good at riding – for a boy," Fizza replied and they ran up the hill together, laughing.

As they walked into a square yard, Fizza looked around her. She could see a line of wood stables and in each stable there was a large horse.

"Watch this," said Fletcher and he put his lips together and whistled[10].

Immediately the horses put their ears up and became very excited. They were obviously happy to see him. However, Fizza moved behind Fletcher because they made her feel nervous.

"It's OK, Fizza, they won't hurt you – they're very gentle," said Fletcher. "These horses have to be large because they pull

the carriages. We have three others that are still out working today."

He put his hand on one of the horses and gently stroked it. Fizza could see that Fletcher loved these horses. Suddenly there was a loud noise behind them. It was the black and white horse and he was kicking his stable door.

"And that's Golden – he recognizes you! He's saying hi!" laughed Fletcher.

"Golden?" replied Fizza. "But he's not golden; he's black and white!"

"Yeah, but don't tell him, he doesn't know that!" he whispered.

Fizza laughed and then pointed at a pretty white horse that had a pink and gray nose.

"Don't tell me – that one's named Chocolate!" she said.

"Don't be stupid – that's Cloudy! Why don't you give her a stroke?"

Very carefully Fizza put out her hand and stroked Cloudy's nose. She was surprised how soft it was.

"She's nice," said Fizza, relaxing a bit.

"Do you want to ride her?" said Fletcher.

Fizza immediately pulled her hand away. She had never ridden a horse before.

"Oh no! Thank you! No, I couldn't! I can't!"

Fletcher smiled at her.

"Come on, Fizza," he said. "Let me teach you."

Chapter 6

The Country Cowboy

Fizza was standing in the middle of a field. Cloudy was on one side of her and Golden was on the other.

"Right," said Fletcher. "First! You have to get on – like this!"

And with a simple little jump, he climbed onto Golden.

"Now, you try."

Nervously, Fizza held onto Cloudy's leather straps and kicked her leg high in the air – unfortunately, at that minute, Cloudy moved and Fizza fell to the ground. Fletcher laughed and laughed. It looked like he was going to fall off his horse.

"No, no, no! You're not *fighting* with her!" he laughed as, with tears in his eyes, he got off Golden.

"Here, let me help you," he said, putting out his hand to help her get up.

Fizza was a bit mad at being laughed at and refused to take it at first.

"Oh, come on!" he said. "Hold the saddle, give me your left leg … and now lift your right leg up and over … whoa! Look out!"

Fizza just missed Fletcher's head as she put her leg in the air, but the next thing she knew, she was sitting on top of Cloudy. Fletcher quickly jumped back on Golden.

"OK! Now!" he said. "Let's go!"

He gave Golden a little kick and they took off across the field very quickly. Fizza's mouth dropped open as she watched them go.

"Is he crazy? I can't do that!" she thought.

However, as Fletcher reached the edge of the field, he turned Golden around and came back to her.

"Why didn't you follow me?" he said, laughing.

Fizza shook her head at him. This guy was crazy … but he was OK.

"I'm not like you! I can't ride like an American cowboy!" she said.

"I can't believe you've never ridden before. So what do you do in Birmingham?"

"I spend my time on my computer, I practice judo, and I go to the shops at the Bullring sometimes."

"The Bullring?"

"Yes, the Bullring Shopping Centre."

"Do you like shopping?"

"Not really, but my friend Babs does."

"Oh, I see," said Fletcher, who couldn't understand why anyone would want to go shopping unless it was for horse food.

"Every cowboy needs a name," he said, "and so I'm going to name you … the Bullring Kid!"

For the next two hours Fletcher McIntyre patiently taught Fizza McIntyre how to ride a horse. They started by walking the horses slowly and, little by little, he got Fizza to go a little faster. Once, when Cloudy went a bit too fast, Fizza became very scared.

"I can't stop!" she screamed. "I can't stop!"

Quickly, Fletcher chased after her, took Cloudy's straps and stopped her. He could see that she was crying.

"It's OK, it's OK, Fizza," he said kindly, "you're doing really well – I won't let you get hurt. I promise."

And Fletcher kept his promise. Very gently and very patiently, he taught Fizza how to ride. By the end of the afternoon her bottom hurt a bit – but she'd had a great time.

"Thank you," she said as they led the horses back to the stables.

"No problem," replied Fletcher. "Umm … what are you doing tomorrow?"

"No plans," said Fizza, suddenly shy. "Why?"

"Well – would you like me to show you some of the island's secrets?"

"Can we go by horse?"

"Is there any other way?" Fletcher replied.

"It's a date!"

As soon as she said it, she realized that she shouldn't have used the word "date."

"I mean, that will be great!" she said quickly, feeling her face go red. She noticed that Fletcher's face was red, too.

"OK," he said. "See you tomorrow."

As Fizza made her way back to the cottage she realized that she hadn't thought of Birmingham or Babs or Billy Adams once all day.

* * *

During the next week Fizza and Fletcher went everywhere together. He showed her how to catch fish with her hands and she showed him her best judo moves. He showed her where the most amazing fish liked to swim and she showed him some clever tricks on his father's very old word processor. They climbed trees and swam in the beautiful clear waters of the Venus Pool. As they explored the island on their horses, Fizza got better and better at riding and she fell in love with Cloudy, the little white horse. Birmingham seemed light years away and they didn't talk about anything else apart from the island … and the fact that their parents all seemed to be getting along so well. Richard had become Rubel and Imran's tour guide, Rubel had become Richard's cook, and Imran had become Richard's judo teacher – whether Richard liked it or not! Fizza didn't know anything about Fletcher's mother. He only mentioned her once, when they were throwing rocks into the sea.

"I haven't seen Dad enjoy himself so much in years – certainly not since Mom left," he said.

"How long ago was that?" asked Fizza.

"When we were in the U.S.," said Fletcher, as he threw a rock angrily into the waves.

Fizza could tell that he didn't want to talk about it, so she changed the subject.

"Well you can thank your dad, because my parents are having a good holiday … and so am I!"

Fletcher smiled at her and jumped up.

"Last one in the sea's a bad egg!" he said.

And Fizza chased him into the sea still wearing her jeans.

*   *   *

One afternoon they explored a dark cave. At first Fizza couldn't see anything, but after a while she began to see things flying around above them.

"What are they?" she asked.

"Bats," said Fletcher. "They live in the dark."

"Urgh! I hate bats," said Fizza just as a small black bat flew straight at her head. She screamed loudly, which scared the bat and it got caught in her hair.

"Agh! Get it off me! Get it off!" she screamed.

"Hey! The Bullring Kid can't be scared of bats – she's much too brave for that!" said Fletcher, laughing.

As he gently put out a hand and picked the bat out of Fizza's hair, the bat immediately became quiet, as if it felt safe in Fletcher's hand. Fizza decided that it was time to leave the cave.

"I think it's time for ice-cream," she said.

"All cowboys need ice-cream!" said Fletcher.

Laughing, they climbed out of the cave and went to untie the horses, which were waiting patiently outside.

Later they sat on the harbor wall eating their ice-cream cones.

"How do you do that?" asked Fizza.

"Do what?" replied Fletcher through a mouthful of strawberry ice-cream.

"How do you get the animals to trust you?"

"I don't know; it just happens."

At that moment a group of "cool" girls walked past. They were the same girls Fizza had seen on the first day of her vacation. They looked at Fletcher and then at Fizza, whispered to one another and disappeared around the corner.

"Do you know them?" asked Fizza.

"Not really. They're in my class in school."

He paused.

"They think I'm strange."

"Why?" asked Fizza.

She suddenly realized that she didn't know anything about Fletcher's school or any of his friends.

"Because I'm different, I suppose. Actually, they call me the Country Cowboy."

"Do you like that?" asked Fizza.

"I don't care really. The conversations I have with animals are much more interesting than talking about the stuff they all talk about … but I like *some* people," he added, looking shyly at her.

Fizza could feel herself turning red again.

"I don't think you can always trust people," he said. "But you can always trust animals."

"Even crazy bats?"

"Even crazy bats!"

At that moment his phone rang.

"Hi, Dad!"

His smile quickly disappeared as he listened to his father.

"What? Are you sure? … OK, I'll be right there."

As he put his phone back into his pocket he turned to Fizza. His bright green eyes were now dark with anger.

"What did I say about not trusting people?"

"What's wrong, Fletcher?" asked Fizza.

"Two of the horses have been stolen."

ACTIVITIES

● ●

1 Check your answer to *Looking forward* on page 17.

2 Complete the sentences with the names in the box.

~~Rubel~~	Fizza (x2)	Fletcher (x3)	Richard (x2)

1 .... *Rubel* .... thinks that Sark is exciting.
2 .... changes her opinion of Sark.
3 .... shows Fizza and her parents the island.
4 .... falls out of a tree.
5 .... has a judo class.
6 .... shows Fizza the island's secrets.
7 .... is the Bullring Kid.
8 .... is the Country Cowboy.

3 <u>Underline</u> the correct word in each sentence.

1 Fizza doesn't buy a newspaper because they *aren't sold /
   hadn't arrived* on Sark.
2 On the first night of the vacation, Fizza sees someone
   watching her from *a tree / a horse*.
3 Fizza doesn't go to the restaurant with her parents because
   she *is tired / has a reason for staying at home*.
4 Fizza *wants / doesn't want* to visit someone who makes pots.
5 Before going to Sark, Fizza *was scared of / didn't like* horses.
6 Her first horseback riding class helps Fizza stop thinking about
   Sark / Birmingham.
7 Fletcher gets *ice-cream / a bat* out of Fizza's hair.

4 What do the <u>underlined</u> words refer to in these lines from the text?

1 "Isn't <u>this</u> exciting, Fizza!" (page 18) *Sark; being on vacation there*

2 "<u>It</u>'s a beautiful little beach" (page 24) ....

3 <u>It</u> was a tall boy wearing jeans (page 26) ....

4 She didn't want to see <u>that rude boy</u>! (page 29)

....

5 "Yeah, but don't tell him, he doesn't know <u>that</u>!" (page 33)

....

6 "I mean, <u>that</u> will be great!" (page 36) ....

7 "How do you do <u>that</u>?" (page 38) ....

5 Answer the questions.

1 Why is Sark "the island that time forgot"?

....

2 How does Fizza feel when she says "It's a date!"? (page 36)

....

3 Why does Fletcher prefer animals to people?

....

4 What happens at the end of Chapter 6?

....

LOOKING FORWARD

• •

6 What do you think? Answer the questions.

1 What do Fizza and Fletcher do to try and get the horses back?

....

2 Fizza takes the blame for something in school – what is it?

....

3 In Chapter 10 there's a new student at Fizza's school – who is it?

....

Chapter 7

Fizza has a plan

"I can't believe it," said Richard McIntyre. "This has never happened before."

Fizza and Fletcher stood beside him. They all stared at the two empty stables.

"Who would steal them, Dad? Who has them?" asked Fletcher angrily.

"Surely they can't be far away?" said Fizza. "Sark's only a small place."

"That's if they're still on the island," said Fletcher.

"Well, you called the police, didn't you?" said Fizza. "They have to search the island immediately!"

"Fizza! This isn't Birmingham!" said Fletcher sharply.

"What Fletcher means is that we only have one part-time officer on the island," interrupted Richard gently.

"Oh, I see," said Fizza.

"And where is he?" asked Fletcher.

"When I called him, he was out fishing – but he's coming back," replied Richard.

Later they heard that other horses had been stolen on the larger islands of Guernsey and Jersey. The Sark policeman arrived at the stables, talked to Richard quietly for a few minutes, and then called the Guernsey police for help.

"Unfortunately," he said when he finished speaking to them, "they are very busy at present, but they promise they will send help as soon as they can."

This was too much for Fletcher, who kicked one of the stable doors angrily.

"That's not good enough!" he shouted.

"Son, we have to be patient," said Richard.

As Fletcher walked out of the yard, Richard looked at Fizza's worried face.

"It's OK, Fizza," he said. "Fletcher doesn't mean it. It's just that he loves these horses – maybe even more than I do. They're more than our business to him – they're his family."

At that moment Fizza's mom and dad arrived. Her dad was carrying a large pan.

"I thought everyone would like some food," said Rubel. "So I've made you all a fish curry!"

"And just when I thought things couldn't get any worse," said Fizza under her breath.

For the first time that afternoon, Richard McIntyre laughed.

* * *

Fizza found Fletcher sitting on a wall, looking down the hill and out to sea, and she sat down beside him. Together, they watched the sun turn from a deep orange to blood red as it dropped out of the sky. Eventually Fletcher made a little noise, which made Fizza turn to look at him. His face was wet with tears.

"Fletcher," she said. "It's going to be OK. I know it is."

"No, it's not!" he said angrily. "It never is! I'm fed up with having things taken away from me!"

"You'll get the horses back, I know you will."

"*She* never came back."

"Who?" Fizza asked.

"Her."

He looked down at his hands.

"Mom."

Fizza looked out to sea. She didn't really know what to say.

She'd always had a mom there for her – she didn't know what it was like not to have a mom. So she decided to keep quiet and listen as Fletcher began to talk. He told Fizza how one day, at the age of twelve, when they all lived in the U.S., he came home from school and found his father crying at the kitchen table. In his large hands he held a note from his wife, Fletcher's mother. It said that she couldn't stay anymore. She needed to leave. And that was that. That morning, Fletcher had seen her for the last time. His parents eventually divorced and so he and his father moved to Sark, away from Colorado, away from the memory of his mother. For the past three years, it had been just him and his dad … and the horses.

"I never spoke to anyone about it before," he said. "I never wanted to."

Fizza looked at him and gave him a little smile. She suddenly felt closer to Fletcher than she had felt to any of her friends, even Babs.

"Thanks," he said, cleaning the tears from his face with his T-shirt.

"Anytime," said Fizza.

They smiled at one another and looked out to sea again.

"Right!" said Fizza suddenly. "We have to get some horses back! And guess what?"

Fletcher sat up and looked at her with his wide, wet green eyes.

"What?" he said.

"I have a plan."

*   *   *

The two fifteen-year-olds led Cloudy into the middle of the field under the dark midnight sky. The little horse's white coat shone under the light of the moon.

44

"It's OK, girl!" whispered Fletcher into her ear as he tied her to a small tree. "We'll watch you!"

Quickly they moved back into the dark corner of the field and left the horse standing alone.

"I can't look at her! She looks so scared!" said Fizza. She was beginning to wish that she hadn't had the idea of leaving a horse out as a trap to catch horse thieves.

However, Fletcher and Fizza hid themselves behind a large tree and watched Cloudy. They had chosen her for this job because of her bright white coat that could easily be seen from a few hundred meters away. An hour went by and nothing happened, and then another. Fizza was getting tired and her eyes were becoming heavy.

"Fletcher!" she whispered. "Should we just give up? This is stupid! It's obvious no one's coming to take her!"

Suddenly Fletcher took hold of her arm.

"Shh!" he said. "Look! What's that?"

On the far side of the field, they could see a small light and Fizza held her breath as it moved toward the little white shape of Cloudy. Soon, they could both see that the light was being carried by a man.

"This is it!" whispered Fletcher.

After a few minutes, the man got to the horse and as quickly as he had appeared, he disappeared into the darkness, taking the little horse with him.

"Poor Cloudy!" said Fizza.

"Come on!" Fletcher whispered as he ran forward to follow them.

As they came to the far edge of the field they looked down the hill toward the moonlit sea. At first they couldn't see anything, but then suddenly Fizza jumped.

"There she is!" she said.

Fletcher looked down the hill and saw, moving along pretty slowly, the unmistakable white shape of Cloudy.

"Come on!" he whispered. "But keep your distance!"

Slowly and as quietly as they could, they followed the horse and her kidnapper for about twenty minutes. They couldn't see where they were going and several times they fell against rocks and bushes. Fizza's feet were beginning to hurt and she was cold. She wished she'd put a warmer sweater on. The sea was on their right but it became hidden when they passed behind some tall trees.

"I think he's taking her down to Derrible Bay," said Fletcher.

They knew the sea was close because they could hear the waves crashing onto a beach. Now Fizza was worried because she hadn't planned what to do next if her plan worked!

"So now what are we supposed to do?" she whispered to Fletcher in the dark.

"It's OK, Fizza," he said. "This time it's *my* turn to have the plan."

And he took his phone out of his pocket.

Chapter 8

Laying a trap

Fletcher and Fizza climbed quietly down the hill a few more meters and looked out carefully from behind a small bush. Cloudy's kidnapper was talking to another man who he had met on the beach. The men were so close that Fizza and Fletcher could hear them speak. In the dark they could see that one was fat and the other one was thin. It was the thin one that had stolen Cloudy.

"Well done! That looks like a nice horse!" the fat man said.

"Yes, we should get a good price for it," replied the thin man. "When's the boat going to get here?"

"Any minute now … I'll get the others," said the fat man.

He disappeared behind some big rocks in a corner of the beach. After a few seconds he came back out of the dark. He was leading two large horses.

"They're our horses!" whispered Fletcher angrily. "Those men have been keeping them here!"

The men were obviously waiting for a boat which would get them off the island. A few minutes later a green light flashed three times out at sea.

"Hey! That's the sign! They're here!" the thin man shouted.

Fizza and Fletcher realized that if they were going to stop these men, they had to act now before help arrived.

"OK, Fizza," whispered Fletcher, "this is what we have to do …"

Seconds later Fizza waited in her position while Fletcher gave a low whistle. All three horses on the sand put their heads up and listened, but the men didn't notice anything. They were too busy looking for their boat. Then Fletcher whistled again and the horses began to jump in excitement. This *did* surprise the men. Every time Fletcher whistled, the horses jumped until they managed to pull their ropes free from the men's hands. Then they began to run in circles around them.

"Catch them, stupid!" shouted one of the men.

"You try! They're too quick!" replied the other one.

This was the moment Fizza was waiting for. She ran onto the beach, jumped in the air, gave a high kick and knocked the fat man down to the ground.

"What's going on?" shouted the thin man. He tried to run and help his friend, but all three horses moved into his way. He couldn't move! Fizza sat on top of the fat man, who lay face down, and held his arms behind his back.

"Ow! That hurts!" he screamed.

"Well, don't move then!" replied Fizza.

She watched as Fletcher tied the thin man's hands and feet together with a rope and then she looked out to sea. The lights from the kidnappers' boat were getting much closer, making the horses run away.

"What are we going to do when that boat gets here?" she asked Fletcher.

"Yeah!" said the fat man through a mouthful of sand. "What *are* you going to do?"

"It's OK," said Fletcher. "It's going to be OK."

In truth, Fletcher was beginning to get a bit worried, too. However, just at that minute they heard a familiar voice.

"Fletcher? Is that you?"

"Dad!"

Richard McIntyre appeared out of the dark. Behind him was Fizza's dad, Imran, and, farther back, two of his carriage drivers.

"There you are!" said Fletcher. "I was beginning to think that you hadn't gotten my message to meet me here!"

Fizza looked at her own father in surprise.

"Dad?" said Fizza. "What are you doing here?"

"I thought you might need some help," replied her father, looking at the helpless fat man, "but now I see that you did learn something from my classes after all!"

"So you've found the horses!" said Richard. "Good job!"

Then he looked serious.

"Fletcher, why didn't you tell me what you were doing?" he said. "These men could be dangerous!"

The thin man nodded his head in agreement, but everyone ignored[11] him.

"It's OK, Dad. Fizza and I had it under control, didn't we, Fizz?"

As Fizza smiled, she noticed that the kidnappers' boat was really close now. She still wasn't sure what was going to happen when it arrived. There could be lots more men! However, just as it arrived on the beach, the boat was flooded[12] with a very bright light.

"Stop! This is the police! Turn off your engine!" a voice shouted through a loudspeaker.

The bright light came from four police boats which had arrived very quietly in the dark water and completely surprised the kidnappers. The police boats made a circle around them and they had no way of escape.

"It looks like our Sark policeman asked his friends from Guernsey to come," said Richard. "He said he would when I called him."

Fizza looked at Fletcher and smiled.

"OK, Country Cowboy?"

"Not bad, Bullring Kid," he replied. "Not bad."

*   *   *

The next day was a good day and a bad one. It was good because Fizza and Fletcher had helped catch the horse thieves. And this had made them local heroes[13]. However, it was bad because it was the last day of Fizza's vacation. It was almost a joke – two weeks ago she hadn't wanted to come to Sark and now she didn't want to leave it!

Richard McIntyre took them to the harbor with their luggage. She watched sadly as he unloaded[14] their luggage from his carriage onto the road. As Imran said good-bye, he promised Richard free judo classes if he came to Birmingham. Then Richard kissed Rubel on the cheek and thanked her for her wonderful fish curry. Then it was Fizza's turn to say good-bye to Fletcher who was sitting on a wall.

"Say good-bye to the horses for me," she said because she didn't want to say good-bye to him. "It's been great. Thanks."

"Yeah," said Fletcher quietly without looking at her, "the best."

Suddenly shy, Fizza climbed sadly onto the boat. But when she turned back, he had gone. And she knew she would probably never see him again.

"He doesn't care I'm going!" she thought. "He didn't even wait for the boat to leave!"

But Fizza McIntyre didn't know the real reason. Fletcher McIntyre had left because, once again, someone was leaving him behind. And that person had become very special to him.

As the boat began its trip across the sea, Fizza's mom and dad waved at Richard until he disappeared from view. Then Fizza's mom turned and smiled at Fizza.

"Do you know something, Fizza?" she said.

Fizza was too miserable to reply at first.

"I think The Richard McIntyre Horse and Carriage Company could be the answer to some of Birmingham's big problems."

"What do you mean?" asked Fizza, staring at the waves.

"Wait and see, Fizza. Wait and see."

Chapter 9

Fizza takes the blame

It was the first day of the fall term and Fizza walked slowly through the school gates.

"Fizza!"

She turned and saw her friend Babs running toward her.

"Fizza! Guess what!"

"What?" said Fizza.

"I'm in love!"

"With Billy?"

"Billy who?" said Babs. "No! It's a wonderful boy I met in Greece. He's named Jake and he's really good-looking! I'm crazy about him!"

And Babs told Fizza all about Jake and where he was from and how they planned to see each other again soon.

"And how was your holiday, Fizza?" she said when she had eventually finished. "How was Sark?"

"Cool," said Fizza. "It was cool."

At that moment Babs's cell phone made a sound.

"Oh!" cried Babs. "It's a text from Jake! Excuse me!"

Fizza smiled. Last term Babs was madly in love with Billy Adams. This term, however, she had forgotten who he was and she was madly in love with someone else.

* * *

Fizza had a surprise that morning and it wasn't a good one. The whole school was in the large auditorium to hear the principal, Mr. Jackson, speak. All the children listened and tried not to yawn, as he talked and talked.

"Now, I have something very serious to say about some very bad behavior last term."

Everyone sat up and listened.

"At the end of last term certain students were responsible for this."

He held up a picture of two of the teachers. One lady teacher had a beard and was wearing men's pants and beside her was a man wearing a dress covered in yellow flowers. Fizza recognized it immediately. It was one of the pictures she had changed for Billy Adams.

"Nobody will be able to use the computer rooms until the person – or people – who did this come and see me in my office," said Mr. Jackson. "Now, all go to your classes, please."

Fizza couldn't move. It was her! Babs looked at her with wide eyes and she could feel the "cool" girls whispering behind her.

"What are you going to do?" whispered Babs.

Fizza knew what she had to do.

"I have to go and see Mr. Jackson," she said.

"But what about Billy Adams? It was his idea!" said Babs.

"But *I* did it," said Fizza. "See you later."

And she left the school auditorium and went to wait outside the principal's office.

* * *

Mr. Jackson looked at Fizza over the top of his glasses. He had Fizza's pictures of the teachers on his desk.

"This is so unlike you, Felicity. Why did you do it?"

"I don't know. I thought it was a funny thing to do, I suppose."

Mr. Jackson shook his head. He was obviously surprised.

"And you did it all on your own?"

Fizza paused. She was not going to give Billy Adams's name, even if it had been his idea.

"Yes, sir," she said, trying not to cry.

"Well, in that case—" began Mr. Jackson, but he was interrupted by a knock on the door.

It was the school secretary.

"I have Billy Adams here. He would like to see you."

As Billy Adams walked into the office, Fizza realized she hadn't seen him since that day in the Bullring Shopping Centre during the vacation. He had a suntan from the summer sunshine and his blond hair was longer and almost white now. Fizza thought he looked more handsome than ever.

"Hi, Billy, can I help you?" asked Mr. Jackson.

"Sir, it was my idea," he said. "The computer trick was all my idea."

He stood looking straight ahead without once looking at Fizza.

"But," Mr. Jackson said, "Felicity said she did it all on her own."

"Well, she's wrong, sir. It was my idea," replied Billy.

"What a great guy," thought Fizza. "He's taking the blame for the whole thing!"

The truth was that Billy Adams felt guilty. The joke on the teachers had been his idea and it wasn't fair if this quiet girl got into trouble for it. Mr. Jackson listened as Billy explained what had happened.

"Billy, I understand that it was your idea, but Felicity shouldn't have helped you," said Mr. Jackson. "It was wrong of both of you."

However, secretly Mr. Jackson was pleased with their honesty. He told them to write a letter of apology to all the teachers in the pictures.

"Now, go back to your classes and if there is any more bad behavior this term, you'll be in trouble."

Outside in the hallway, Fizza was just about to walk away, but Billy stopped her.

"Thank you," he said. "You didn't need to take the blame."

"Yes, I did," said Fizza. "I did it, too."

Billy took a closer look at Fizza. He couldn't believe that this was the same girl who had helped him with the pictures at the end of the last term. She was so different! She was so confident! And he hadn't realized she was so pretty!

*   *   *

Fizza's mom was waiting for her in the kitchen when she got home from school. She looked serious.

"Hi, Fizza," she said. "I had a phone call today ..."

"Oh no," thought Fizza. "It had to have been Mr. Jackson! Now my mother's going to be angry with me!"

"And I have to say—" said her mom.

Fizza waited to be told off.

"—that something very exciting is going to happen in Birmingham soon! But it has to be a secret! I can't tell you until it's final!"

And then her mom jumped around the kitchen in excitement.

"What is it?" asked Fizza, laughing.

"Oh, I can't tell you! I wish I could, but it's Council business! And all things have to be done correctly."

"Can't you tell me anything?" asked Fizza.

"OK," said her mom. "I'll say two words: 'horses' and 'carriages'!"

And it didn't matter how many questions Fizza asked her mom, she wouldn't tell her anymore.

"Anyway," she said, changing the subject. "How was your first day back at school?"

Fizza was just wondering if she should tell her mom about getting into trouble with Mr. Jackson when the phone rang.

"I'll get it!" she said as she ran for the phone.

"Hello?" she said.

"Fizza?" a boy's voice said.

"Yes?"

"Fizza, it's Billy. Billy Adams."

Fizza's heart gave a little jump.

"Oh, hi," she said, trying her best to sound cool.

"I wondered if you'd like to come to the park."

"When?"

"This evening?"

An hour later Fizza found herself walking through the park with Billy Adams. What a crazy day it had been! She had started the day feeling really miserable and she was ending the day feeling wonderful! As they walked, they talked about school, family, and friends. He told her how he loved soccer and playing his guitar, and she told him about her judo.

"Show me a move then!" said Billy.

And so Fizza threw him over her back and onto the ground and this made them laugh a lot.

"Where did you learn to do that?" he said as he lay on the grass.

"My dad taught me!" laughed Fizza.

"Well, tell him I want some classes!"

Then they began to talk about their vacations in the summer and Fizza told him all about her adventures on Sark, the horses, and Fletcher.

"So was it a holiday romance?" asked Billy.

Fizza laughed.

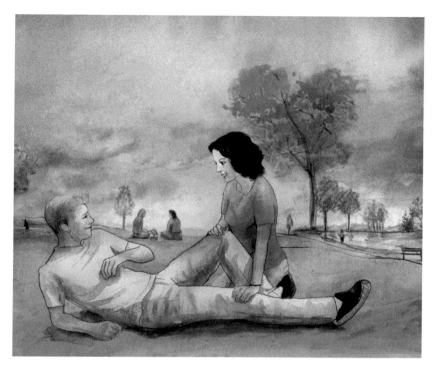

"No! Of course not! He was just a really good friend!"

As it began to get dark, Billy walked her home.

"Would you like to do this again?" he asked her as they stood outside her house.

"Yes. That would be nice," she replied.

"What about tomorrow evening? Are you free?"

"Yes. I'm free," she said.

Suddenly her vacation on Sark seemed like a very long time ago.

Chapter 10

A new student

Two weeks later Fizza walked through the school gates.

"Fizza!"

She turned and saw Babs running toward her.

"Fizza! Is it true?"

"Is what true?"

"Are you going out with Billy Adams?"

Fizza laughed.

"What? No! Of course not! He's just a friend."

"Hmm," said Babs.

It was obvious Babs didn't believe her.

In the two weeks since the beginning of term, Fizza had spent a lot of time with Billy. They had been to the park and the movie theater, and he'd even been to her house and her dad had taught him some judo moves. But they hadn't held hands or kissed! She wasn't shy of him anymore, but they weren't girlfriend and boyfriend, they were just friends.

"You know everyone at school is talking about you?" said Babs.

Fizza did know. She had noticed the "cool" girls whispering about her, but she had tried to ignore them.

"Let them talk!" laughed Fizza.

But Babs didn't laugh because, although she had met Jake on vacation, she was a bit jealous of Fizza's relationship with Billy. After all, she had said that she liked him first!

* * *

Fizza was late for class because she had to take some books back to the library. As she walked through the classroom door, she stopped in surprise because, sitting at one of the front desks, was a red-haired boy with green eyes and freckles. It was Fletcher McIntyre.

"Hi, Fizza," he said.

At first Fizza couldn't speak. She just stood with her mouth open. This had to have been her mom's "secret"!

"Fletcher?" she said. "What are you doing here?"

Immediately, all the "cool" girls began to whisper. Then the teacher told Fizza to sit down and class began.

At recess Fizza and Fletcher sat in a corner of the playground so that they could talk. Fletcher explained that his dad had been offered a job by Birmingham City Council.

"You mean my mother offered him a job!" said Fizza.

"I guess so," said Fletcher.

"What is it?"

"It's a 'green' taxi service," he explained. "He's brought the horses and carriages from Sark."

Fizza had a hundred questions.

"Where are you living? Is Cloudy here? Where are the horses?"

Fletcher explained that his father had rented a house and stables in Birmingham.

"We were really lucky to get it," he said. "Apparently there's a man with a factory next door who also wants the land. He wants to build on it, or something."

"So you've brought the countryside to the city!" laughed Fizza. "Well, you showed me the secrets of Sark; now it's my turn to show you the secrets of this school!"

And so that morning Fizza took Fletcher around the school and his wide green eyes grew even wider as she showed him all the different classrooms and hallways. She watched him as he stared everywhere in astonishment[15], and she laughed as he ran out of the way to let the crowds of students pass as they went from class to class.

"There are more people in this school than in all of Sark!" he whispered.

Fizza introduced Fletcher to her friends. She told them that he knew more about the countryside and animals than anyone else she knew. He was amazing! However, not everyone felt the same as Fizza.

"Who is he?" whispered Babs, thinking that he needed a good haircut.

"He's my friend from Sark!" said Fizza.

"He speaks funny."

"He lived in America when he was younger."

"Isn't he a bit …"

"What?"

"You know … strange," said Babs. "He jumps every time an ambulance goes past the school!"

"You don't know him!" said Fizza.

"And where did he get those shoes? They're awful!"

"Oh, just shut up, Babs!"

Fizza thought of how he rode horses, caught fish with his hands, and climbed the highest trees. Babs didn't know how wonderful Fletcher was, because she hadn't seen him do these things!

As the bell rang for the end of school, Fletcher asked Fizza if she wanted to come and see the horses that evening.

"I'd love to!" said Fizza.

Richard McIntyre was waiting to pick Fletcher up at the school gates and he waved at Fizza. Fizza thought it was such fun to see a horse and carriage outside the school!

"See you later!" said Fletcher as he ran happily over to his dad and climbed up on the carriage. Fizza suddenly realized that other students were laughing at him. Some girls from her class, including Babs, walked past her.

"Is 'horse boy' your brother?" asked one.

"No, why?" said Fizza.

"Well, you're both called McIntyre."

Fizza didn't answer.

"I think he's her boyfriend!" said Babs and they all laughed and walked away.

Fizza watched them go. What was wrong with Babs? Why was she being so unkind, too?

* * *

Later, just as Fizza was getting ready to go to see Fletcher and the horses at the stables, the bell rang. Fizza answered the door and found Billy standing on the step.

"Hi, Fizza. Are you ready?" he said.

"Am I ready for what?"

"The movie theater! We arranged it last week! I have the tickets!" he said.

"Oh yes! Of course!" lied Fizza. She had completely forgotten.

As she ran to get her coat, she hoped that Fletcher wouldn't care if she didn't go to the stables that evening.

* * *

The next day Fizza felt extremely guilty as she ran into school. She saw Fletcher sitting in a corner of the playground reading a book.

"Fletcher! I'm so sorry I couldn't come to the stables last night. I had lots of homework," she lied.

"It doesn't matter," he said.

"Maybe I could come tonight?"

"If you want to," he said and he went back to reading his book.

Later, at recess, just as Fizza was trying to talk to Fletcher again, Billy came over.

"Hi, Fizza," he said.

"Fletcher, this is Billy. Billy, this is Fletcher, from Sark ... well, he was from America first, then Sark!" she said.

"Hi, Fletcher," said Billy.

But Fletcher ignored him and turned his head away. Fizza looked at him. He was behaving just like he had the first time she had met him on Sark: rude, bad-tempered, *unlikeable*. Not like Billy. The previous evening she had had a nice time with Billy at the movie theater – as she always did.

"Didn't we have a great time last night?" said Billy.

Fletcher turned and stared angrily at Fizza. Now he knew the real reason why she had not gone to the stables. Fizza tried to smile at him, but he just walked toward a tree, climbed it and sat on the highest branch he could find.

"Is he OK?" asked Billy. "He's a bit—"

"What?" replied Fizza sharply.

"You know ... strange?" said Billy, who didn't like Fizza's relationship with this odd boy. Why couldn't he go back to Sark?

"He's not strange!" said Fizza. "He's great! He's just arrived here, that's all!"

By then other students had started laughing at the new red-haired boy who had climbed the tree. And they laughed even more when the school cat climbed up and sat with him.

"Poor Fletcher," thought Fizza. "I should have gone to see him last night! He doesn't know anyone in all of Birmingham! What sort of friend am I?"

At the end of the day, Fizza saw Fletcher walking out of the school gates. He didn't look very happy.

"Fletcher! Wait!"

But he carried on walking.

"Fletcher! I'll come over to the stables later, should I?" she said as she ran along beside him.

"If you want, but don't you have a date with your boyfriend?" he said.

Suddenly Fizza realized that Fletcher was jealous.

"No, I don't and he's not my boyfriend!" she replied just as Billy Adams walked past them.

"Hi, Fizza," Billy said, making sure he had his back to Fletcher. "What are you doing later?"

"It doesn't matter," interrupted Fletcher.

"I wasn't talking to you, country boy!" Billy replied.

This was too much for Fletcher, who jumped on top of Billy and began to hit him as hard as he could. In return, Billy kicked him and before Fizza knew what was happening, the two boys were in a terrible fight.

"Stop it!" she said. "Please!"

However, they continued to fight, so she took Billy's left arm, held it behind his back and pulled him away from Fletcher. Then she gave Fletcher one of her best kicks and knocked him to the ground.

"Ow!" said Billy.

"Oomph!" screamed Fletcher.

"I said 'Stop it!'" said Fizza as she walked away.

Why couldn't she like two boys at once? Surely she didn't have to choose? For months, years even, nothing had ever happened to Fizza McIntyre. Now everything was happening at once and she wasn't sure if she liked it.

LOOKING BACK

. . . .

1 Check your answers to *Looking forward* on page 41.

2 Are the sentences true (*T*) or false (*F*)?
1 Only one policeman works on Sark. ☐ T
2 Fletcher hasn't seen his mom for ten years. ☐
3 The men are going to kill the horses. ☐
4 Richard called the police in Guernsey and told them to come to Sark. ☐
5 Mr. Jackson is surprised that it was Fizza who changed the pictures. ☐
6 Rubel shares lots of secret information from her work with Fizza. ☐
7 A new student arrives in Fizza's class. ☐
8 Fizza forgets an arrangement she made. ☐

3 <u>Underline</u> the correct words in each sentence.
1 Horses were stolen from *two / <u>three</u>* islands.
2 Fizza and Fletcher use Cloudy because she's a *light color / good horse*.
3 *Fizza / Fletcher* stops the fat man who is trying to steal Cloudy.
4 At the end of the vacation, Fizza *wants / doesn't want* to leave Sark.
5 Fizza and Billy have to *talk / write* to their teachers to say sorry.
6 Fizza takes a walk in the park with *Babs / Billy*.
7 Fletcher finds being in his new school *difficult / easy*.
8 *A teacher / Fizza* stops the fight between Billy and Fletcher.

4 What do the <u>underlined</u> words refer to in these sentences from the text?

1 "I've never spoken to anyone about <u>it</u> before," (page 44)
2 "That's the sign! <u>They</u>'re here!" (page 47)
3 And <u>this</u> had made them local heroes. (page 50)
4 "<u>It</u> was cool." (page 52)
5 "Sir, <u>it</u> was my idea," (page 54)
6 "<u>That</u> would be nice," (page 57)
7 "We were really lucky to get <u>it</u>," (page 59)
8 she wasn't sure if she liked <u>it</u>. (page 63)

5 Answer the questions.

1 Why did Fletcher's mom leave?

2 How does Fizza think that Fletcher feels about her leaving Sark?

3 What do Fizza's friends think of Fletcher?

4 Why do you think Fletcher and Billy fight?

LOOKING FORWARD

6 Check (✓) what you think happens in the final chapters.

1 Fizza chooses Billy to be her boyfriend. ☐
2 Fletcher goes back to Sark to live. ☐
3 Fizza goes to Sark to live. ☐

Chapter 11

Bad neighbors and good friends

Fletcher and Fizza got off the bus in the center of Birmingham. All around them were tall buildings and trucks, buses, and cars that queued past them.

"Where are they, then?" Fizza shouted in an attempt to be heard over the noise of the traffic.

"What?"

"The stables! Where are they?"

"Over there!" shouted Fletcher, pointing at an ugly gray wall which had an old wood gate in the center of it. Fizza could just see the tops of the stables on the other side and a small stone house. Next door to the stables was a large factory with the words "Scully's Waste" written in large, red letters on its roof. Several of the factory's trucks were parked right beside it. Fizza was very much a city girl, but even she hadn't expected this. To her, stables should be in the middle of the country, just like they had been on Sark. It seemed crazy to find them in the middle of a city!

"You're joking!" she said. "You must hate it here!"

"It's OK once you get inside," said Fletcher. "Come on. Oh, and please don't mention the fight – Dad will go crazy."

"Only if you don't tell my mom that I joined in!" she replied. "She's meeting me here."

Smiling, Fletcher opened the large, wood gate and they stepped into the yard. He was right: once they were inside the wall it didn't feel that different from the stables on Sark. The first thing Fizza saw was a line of stables and in each stable there was a horse. They were the same kind faces that she had loved when she was on vacation on Sark and they all turned to say hi. Then Fizza heard someone kicking against a stable door.

"I know who that is!" she said.

And she had guessed right, because in a corner of the yard was a handsome black and white horse.

"Hi, Golden!" laughed Fizza as she went over to him. Then she saw Cloudy and ran over to her to stroke her nose.

"Oh! Cloudy! It's so good to see them all again!" she cried.

"Yeah. They think it's good to see you, too," said Fletcher.

At that moment Fletcher's dad came out of the house followed by Fizza's mom. They were both holding mugs of tea.

"It's Miss Fizza McIntyre! The judo kid who saved my horses!" he screamed.

Fizza smiled. She really liked Fletcher's dad. He was always so happy.

"It's Mr. Richard McIntyre! The man who's brought a little bit of Sark to Birmingham to make it greener!" she replied. "How's the taxi service?"

"Well, it's only just started but hopefully it's going to be OK!" said Richard.

"I know it's going to be very successful!" said Fizza's mom. "So how was school?"

"Great!" lied Fizza and Fletcher together.

"Have you made lots of new friends, Fletcher?" asked Richard.

Luckily, before Fletcher could answer his dad, he was interrupted by the loud noise of several engines. All of the Scully's Waste trucks had started up at once. Then the drivers began to sound their horns over and over again. For the first time ever, Fizza saw Richard McIntyre get mad.

"Why do they keep doing that?" he asked. "It's the fourth time they've done it in an hour. They're scaring the horses!"

"I told you, Richard," said Fizza's mom. "It's Robert Scully. He owns the factory and he's annoyed the City Council has given this land to you and not to him. He likes getting what he wants! He's already complained to the Council. He'll relax, I'm sure."

Cloudy was shaking her head. The poor horse didn't like the noise at all. Suddenly they saw a short man standing at the gate. He had gray hair combed back from his red face and wore a brown suit.

"Sorry, McIntyre. Are my trucks making too much noise?"

Fizza and Fletcher immediately knew who it was. It had to be Robert Scully.

"Well, they *are* scaring the horses—" began Richard.

"Sorry! My drivers can be very naughty sometimes!" replied Scully and he walked away, laughing.

Fizza and Fletcher looked at one another. They didn't like Robert Scully at all.

*   *   *

The next morning Fizza met Fletcher just as he got off the bus outside the school.

"Hi, Fizza," he said.

"Hi, Fletcher. Did Robert Scully's trucks make any more noise last night?"

"No, but we heard them all go out early this morning."

"Well, hopefully my mother's right – he'll relax soon."

"Yeah, I hope so."

As they walked through the gates, they saw Billy Adams coming in the opposite direction.

"Oh no, look who it is," said Fletcher.

"Oh, Fletcher, can't you try to be friends with him?"

"I don't want to be his friend," replied Fletcher.

"I think that you two would be good friends. He's OK really."

Fletcher paused and looked at her.

"OK," he said, "I'll try. Just for you."

Fizza smiled at Fletcher. She knew how difficult this had to be for him, especially as he was the new boy. A few seconds later, as Billy Adams walked around the corner, Fletcher was waiting for him.

"Um. Hi, Billy," he began.

Billy stopped. He had a cookie in his hand and he was chewing.

"Yeah?" he said.

"I just wanted to say that I'm sorry for fighting with you," said Fletcher.

However, Fletcher realized that Billy wasn't looking at him because he was staring right past him. Fletcher was beginning to find it difficult to be patient.

"Look, Billy, I'm trying to be friendly here, but if you don't want to be …"

Without saying another word, Billy began to run toward the school.

"I'm not that scary, am I?" Fletcher asked an equally surprised Fizza.

At that moment, a big black dog ran past them. But it didn't run past Billy – it chased him.

"Do you think it's after what Billy's eating?" asked Fizza.

"I don't know – whatever it is, it doesn't look very friendly!" said Fletcher as he dropped his bag and ran after the dog.

Billy jumped up onto a wall and ran along it but the angry dog ran along beside him. Billy was cornered. The dog stared up at him, showed its teeth and began to growl[16]. It did not like poor scared Billy at all.

"It's OK, Billy!" whispered Fletcher. "Throw your cookie on the ground!"

Immediately, Billy threw the half-eaten cookie onto the grass. The dog ate it, but still seemed to be interested in Billy.

By now a crowd of students had gathered[17] and were watching in excitement. Very slowly Fletcher bent down and called softly to the dog.

"Here, boy!"

The dog turned and began to move toward Fletcher. For a moment it looked like it was going to attack him, too.

"It's OK, boy, come here …" said Fletcher gently.

Suddenly the dog dropped its ears, put its head down, and walked over to Fletcher.

"Good boy!" said Fletcher, holding onto the dog. "Good boy!"

As soon as he knew he was safe, Billy jumped off the wall.

"Thanks, Fletcher," he said quietly.

"It's OK," replied Fletcher.

Fizza came over to join them.

"Right," she said. "Let's start again, can we?"

The two boys laughed.

"Billy, this is Fletcher. Fletcher, this is Billy," she said.

"Hi, Fletcher," said Billy, smiling.

"Hi, nice to meet you, Billy," replied Fletcher.

Chapter 12

A message for the McIntyres

Soon the story of Fletcher McIntyre saving Billy Adams from a crazy dog was hot news all through the school. Fletcher became a hero.

Fizza watched happily as Fletcher joined Billy and his friends in a game of soccer.

Even Babs suddenly became very interested in Fletcher and she spent the whole math class asking him about his horses.

"How interesting!" she said when he told her about his dad's new taxi service. "I'd love to come and see them!"

Fizza listened to their conversation. Babs didn't even like horses! Then she heard some of the other girls talking about him.

"He's kind of handsome," whispered one.

"Yeah," replied her friend, "but he'd be even better-looking if he wore better clothes!"

"Well, girls, should we take him shopping tonight?" Babs called out to them.

"Yeah!"

"Is that OK with you, Fletcher?" asked Babs through her pretty, long eyelashes.

"Uh, yeah. Sure!" smiled Fletcher.

"Can we take one of your dad's taxis?"

"OK!"

At the end of the day, Fizza watched as Fletcher, Babs, and two other girls climbed excitedly into one of Richard McIntyre's carriages. Babs hadn't even asked her if she wanted to join them! Fizza suddenly felt very lonely and realized that she was jealous. She didn't know if she was jealous of Babs, or if she was jealous that Fletcher was having a good time without her.

"It's not fair!" she thought. "Fletcher McIntyre is *my* friend!"

As the carriage pulled away, Fletcher saw her standing by the school gate and stood up.

"Fizza! Aren't you coming?" he shouted.

"No, thanks! I have better things to do!" she replied.

"She has 'better things to do,' Fletcher!" said Babs in a funny voice as she pulled him back down.

Fizza couldn't believe that Babs was being so mean to her! Miserably, she watched the carriage full of laughing girls and Fletcher drive away. However, even before they'd disappeared from view, Fizza knew that she was being stupid. She should be pleased that Fletcher was happy in school now.

"Stop being so selfish, Fizza McIntyre!" she said to herself.

She decided to go and see him at the stables later.

* * *

After tea, when Fizza arrived at the stables, she found the large gate in the wall had been left open. She stopped before she entered the yard.

"Hello! Is anyone in? It's me! Fizza!" she shouted.

Since there was no reply, she gently pushed the gate open wide. She noticed that a few of the stables were empty and several of the carriages had gone.

"Richard's taxi service is having a busy day," she thought.

Then she looked farther into the yard. There was no sign of Fletcher, who was probably still out shopping with the girls. She smiled as she wondered if Fletcher was enjoying himself.

Then suddenly she stopped smiling because she realized something was wrong. Something was very wrong. Quickly she looked around at all the stables and what she saw made her feel sick. A message had been written in red paint on every door.

"Get out!"

"Go back to Sark!"

"Leave … or it's horse on the menu!"

Fizza put her hand to her mouth and stared at the words. This was horrible!

"Oh my goodness!" she thought. "I hope the horses are OK!"

Quickly she ran from stable to stable and saw that Cloudy, Golden, and the other horses were safe. Then she called Fletcher on her cell phone. After a couple of rings he answered.

"Fizza! You should be here! They're trying to make me wear pink!" he laughed.

Fizza could hear girls' laughter behind him.

"Fletcher. You have to come back to the stables. Now!"

There was a pause.

"Why?" he asked, his voice suddenly serious.

Fizza took a deep breath.

"Someone's left you a message."

* * *

The next day after school Fizza, Fletcher, and Billy sat in her yard discussing what had happened at the stables.

"Dad's really upset[18]," said Fletcher.

"I'm not surprised! But he's not thinking of leaving Birmingham, is he?" asked Fizza.

"I don't know. He's worried that if it happens again, the horses could get hurt."

"So, do you think it was Robert Scully?" asked Fizza.

"I don't think – I *know* it was Robert Scully – or one of his men," said Fletcher.

"But the police say that there's nothing to show that it was him."

"Scully's not a nice man," said Billy. "My dad used to be one of his drivers years ago."

"I'd love to do something to Scully," said Fizza.

They all sat and thought for a while.

"Should we go and write messages on his trucks?" suggested Billy.

"No," said Fizza. "We can do better than that."

"Oh, yeah?" said Fletcher.

Fizza nodded her head.

"What did your dad think of Scully, Billy?" she asked.

"He hated him. He thought that Scully had secrets – but Scully got rid of him before he could find out what they were," replied Billy.

"Well, let's find them!" said Fizza excitedly.

"And how are we going to do that?" asked Billy.

"Operation Scully!" Fizza replied.

After a couple of hours Fizza and the boys had worked out a plan and Fizza typed it onto a piece of paper. It read:

OPERATION SCULLY
TIME: TUESDAY, EIGHT O'CLOCK
1. *Scully will be interviewed for "school magazine" at his house about being a successful factory owner in Birmingham*
2. *Fletcher and Billy will search Scully's office*
3. *Fizza will search Scully's e-mail for secrets*

The bell rang and Fizza went to answer the door. She discovered Babs, holding a big box of chocolates.

"Oh, hi, Babs," said Fizza.

The two girls hadn't spoken since Babs had taken Fletcher shopping the day before. Babs held up a piece of paper and began to read.

"Fizza. I haven't been nice to you. I was jealous of you and Billy and then I was jealous of you and Fletcher. You seemed to be having such a good time without me, so I tried to get Fletcher to like me instead of you. But I feel bad now—"

"OK, Babs! It's OK!" interrupted Fizza.

However, Babs hadn't finished.

"And I was hurt because Jake had stopped calling me. He's met someone else! Sorry."

Fizza held her arms out to Babs.

"Oh, Babs, come in!" she said. "I have a job for you!"

*   *   *

At first Babs wasn't sure about going to Scully's house to interview him.

"But why do *I* have to interview him?" she asked.

"Because we need him out of the way so that we can search his factory," replied Fletcher.

"But I don't work for the school magazine!" said Babs.

"He won't know that," said Fletcher.

"But I'm … I'm bad at things like that!" said Babs.

"Babs," said Billy, putting his hand on her arm and smiling at her. His blond hair shone in the Sunday afternoon sunshine and he looked more handsome than ever. "Of course you can do it – because you're the best."

Babs looked at him and turned a little red.

"Oh, all right then," she said.

Chapter 13

Scully is shy of cameras

For two hours on Tuesday evening Fizza sat at her computer in her bedroom. She was trying to get into Scully's computer in his office so that she could read his e-mails. However, she just couldn't find his secret password. The phone rang. It was Babs.

"Fizza!" Babs whispered. "I've locked myself in Robert Scully's bathroom! Have you managed to get into his computer yet?"

"Not yet! You'll have to keep Scully busy! How's the interview going?"

"Oh! He really likes himself!" said Babs. "He's talked for two hours about how rich he is and how many cars he has … and his wife is yucky! Everything about her is false! Her hair, her nails, probably her teeth! And her skirts are too short – she's the same age as my mother, for goodness' sake[19]! And she has this stupid little dog that she carries everywhere—"

Fizza suddenly interrupted her.

"What's its name?"

"Oh … Bubble Gum. That's it. That's a stupid name, too."

Fizza typed in the words "Bubble Gum." Immediately she got into Robert Scully's e-mails.

"Babs. You're great!"

"Oh, am I?" said Babs. "Thanks."

Fizza started to look through the e-mails in Robert Scully's computer. She'd never done this before and she was scared.

What if she got caught? She'd be in big trouble with Scully. And the police! She knew she had to work quickly.

"OK, Babs! You have to keep him talking – I don't want him anywhere near his computer while I'm in there!"

"Oh, I wouldn't worry about that – he's on the phone to the police right now."

Fizza immediately stopped working on her computer.

"The police? Why?"

"Oh, they called him because some robbers have broken into his factory or something."

"Did they catch them?"

"I don't know – why would I care?" said Babs.

"Because those 'robbers' would have been Fletcher and Billy."

"Oh."

However, as she finished her call with Babs, Fizza's cell phone immediately rang again. It was Fletcher.

"Fletcher?" she said. "Babs said the police called Scully! Are you OK?"

"Yeah … but it was close! Billy and I got out just as the police arrived!"

"Did you find anything?" she asked.

"Yeah! Several cans of red paint!" said Fletcher.

As she listened, Fizza worked at her computer searching through Scully's e-mails.

"And did you manage to get into Scully's e-mails?" asked Fletcher.

"Yes!" replied Fizza.

"Well? Did you find anything?"

"Oh, yes, Fletcher McIntyre. I think I just did."

* * *

The next evening Fizza and Fletcher rode Golden and Cloudy out of the center of Birmingham. Soon the buildings disappeared and it became greener.

"So tell me again what that e-mail said," said Fletcher.

"It was an e-mail to all his drivers. It said if the other rubbish[20] areas were full, they had to take all the rubbish to the Park Hill area – at night," replied Fizza.

"So he doesn't want anyone to see him doing that then?"

"No, because he's breaking the law! He isn't getting rid of rubbish in the proper places!"

"And he's getting paid for it. No wonder he's a millionaire!" said Fletcher.

"So now we have to catch him actually doing it!" said Fizza, taking a new cell phone out of her pocket.

"What? With a phone?"

"Yes, it's my mother's new phone, but it's really good for recording videos!"

"And does your mom know you have it?"

"No. And she won't because I'll put it back later. I've just borrowed it."

Eventually they came to a sign above a gate saying: "Park Hill – the heart of a greener Birmingham."

The gate led them into a large, open green field. There were tall trees all around it. Fizza and Fletcher quickly rode toward the trees to hide. They didn't know how long they'd have to wait. But they hoped that one of Scully's trucks would make an appearance that evening.

* * *

It was just getting dark when Fletcher shook Fizza's arm. Fizza opened her eyes; they'd been waiting so long, she had to have gone to sleep.

"Look!" he whispered.

Fizza looked in the direction where Fletcher was pointing. In the poor light she could just about see the shape of a large truck. It was moving very slowly across the large green space.

"They're here!"

There was no mistake about it: it was one of Scully's trucks. As quickly as she could, Fizza took her mom's phone out of her pocket, held it up and pressed the "record" button. The truck stopped, its back went up into the air and a huge pile of garbage was dropped onto the ground.

"Got them!" said Fizza.

Then, suddenly, the phone began to ring.

"Turn it off!" whispered Fletcher. "They'll hear it!"

Fizza looked at the phone. It said the call was from "Home."

"OK!" Fizza replied, but then she decided to answer it in case it was urgent.

"Hello?" she said.

"Fizza? Is that you? What are you doing with my new phone?"

It was her mom!

"Sorry! I can't talk now! I'll call you later!"

And she hit the "off" button. Now her mom knew that she had taken her phone!

"I'm in trouble now," she thought.

But when she heard the truck drivers shouting, she realized that they were in even bigger trouble.

"Who's there?"

"It's two kids!"

"Quick!" said Fletcher. "Let's get back to the horses!"

They ran over to the tree where Golden and Cloudy were waiting for them.

"Follow me!" said Fletcher as he jumped up on Golden and began to ride across the grass. Fizza told herself to be brave and she followed Fletcher as quickly as she could. As they passed the truck, three big men appeared out of the dark and began to run toward them.

"Come on, girl," said Fizza to Cloudy. "We can do it!"

As the men reached out for her, Cloudy suddenly jumped up. Fizza was almost thrown to the ground, but she just managed to hang on. Then the little horse began to move as fast as her legs would take her across the field and up the road.

"We've lost them!" said Fizza.

"Great!" cried Fletcher.

Eventually, feeling safer, they rode a little more slowly. Fletcher turned and noticed that Fizza had almost stopped.

"Are you OK, Fizza?" he asked.

"Yeah. I'm trying to send a text to Babs," she said.

This annoyed Fletcher.

"Why do girls always have to send messages to one another – whatever is happening?" he said.

"Because we need a plan!" said Fizza.

Just then they heard the noise of an engine coming up behind them. As she turned to see what it was, Fizza almost dropped the phone.

"That was close!" she thought. "My mother would have gone crazy!"

The vehicle came closer and they saw that it was the garbage truck. It was following them!

"Actually, we need a plan right now!" said Fletcher.

He kicked Golden to move more quickly and Fizza, who was beginning to miss her nice warm bed at home, followed him. And they had the ride of their lives through the streets of Birmingham. They went down major roads and down small streets, around roundabouts and under bridges. But the truck just kept following them. At one point a night bus suddenly appeared; it made Golden jump and Fletcher almost fell to the ground. Eventually he led them up a path that was too small for the truck and it couldn't follow any farther. At the end of the path Fizza could see the stables! They were safe at last! Quickly they rode into the yard, jumped off the horses, and ran into the house.

They found Richard McIntyre sitting at the kitchen table. He looked worried.

"Fletcher! Fizza!" he said. "Where have you been?"

"It's OK, Richard!" said Fizza. "We have a video that shows what Scully has been doing!"

"Yes, and if there's any more trouble from him, we'll take it to the police!" said Fletcher.

At that moment, someone else stepped forward from a dark corner of the room.

"Fletcher! It's good to see you! Your poor father has been worried about you. Well, now that you're here – you can show me that video too, can't you?"

Fizza and Fletcher turned to see Robert Scully standing behind them.

Chapter 14

Big business for the McIntyres

Scully looked at Fletcher and Fizza with his hard eyes.

"I heard you were up on Park Hill," he said. "So I thought I'd come and have a cup of tea with your dad while we waited for you."

"Well, we're back now – so you can go," said Fletcher.

"No, I can't, young man. Not until I have your camera."

"We don't have a camera," said Fletcher.

"That's funny," replied Scully. "My drivers said you had a camera and that you were filming my truck!"

Fletcher and Fizza stared at him. It was Richard who spoke next.

"Come on, kids, give the camera to Mr. Scully," he said gently. "I think it will only make things worse if you don't."

Fizza took out her mom's cell phone and put it on the table.

"It isn't a camera," she said. "It's a phone, actually."

"Nice," said Scully. "This phone is very expensive."

Then as Fizza watched, Scully picked up the phone and dropped it into a mug of tea on the table in front of him.

"Now there's no more video. Actually, there's no more phone!"

Fizza couldn't believe what he'd done. He'd destroyed her mom's phone. Her mom was going to go crazy!

"That's my mother's! How could you?"

Scully ignored her and stood up to leave.

"Right, I'll say good night then and just so that you don't

do anything stupid, I think I'll borrow something – to remind you to behave."

"Like what?" said Richard.

"Well, what about one of your horses? I think I'll take that nice black and white one home."

"Golden? You can't! We'll call the police!" said Fletcher.

"Well, if you do, it might be the last time you see him."

And so Richard, Fizza, and Fletcher watched as two of Scully's men pulled Golden into the back of a white van. Golden kicked them as hard as he could.

"Go on, boy! Get them!" shouted Fletcher.

As Golden was finally driven away in the back of the van, another of Scully's drivers parked a truck in front of the stable gate. It meant that Richard's carriages couldn't leave the stables.

"Just in case you get any stupid ideas!" said Scully, laughing. He got into his car and drove off into the night.

As they watched Scully disappear, the three of them felt completely helpless.

"I'm going to follow him!" said Fletcher.

"Hold on!" said his father. "Let's not do anything that might put Golden in danger!"

Fletcher fell into an angry silence. Then Fizza suddenly remembered something.

"Oh! How could I be so stupid!" she exclaimed.

Fletcher and Richard looked at her in surprise.

"Richard, did you check your e-mails tonight?" she asked.

"No. I was a little busy!" he replied.

"Well, you have time to look now!"

*   *   *

A few minutes later Richard came back, smiling.

"Fizza McIntyre, you are one smart girl," he laughed.

"What has she done?" asked Fletcher.

"She e-mailed me the video of Scully's truck on Park Hill from her mom's phone!"

It meant they still had the video that could be used against Scully!

"Now what do we do?" asked Fletcher, but before anyone could reply they were interrupted by a taxi stopping outside. Billy and Babs got out.

"I got your text!" said Babs.

"What's happened?" asked Billy.

Fizza and Fletcher explained as quickly as they could.

"Poor Golden!" said Babs.

"Well, I think the police would love to see a copy of that video, don't you?" said Richard.

"You do that, Dad, but I'm going to get Golden back from Scully's house!" said Fletcher.

"I know where he lives!" said Babs.

"OK!" said Billy. "Let's go!"

"We can't! We can't get the carriages out because of the truck!" said Fizza.

"Oh, don't worry about that," said Billy, climbing up and looking into the garbage truck. Everyone stared at him.

"Did I mention that my dad is a truck driver?" he shouted. "He often leaves the keys in his truck – and *they've* left them, too!"

He started the engine.

"But that's stealing!" said Babs.

"I'm not stealing it!" he laughed. "I'm just moving it. And then we can get the carriages out."

*   *   *

"This is the best!" said Billy, as Fletcher drove the horse and carriage through the quiet streets of Birmingham.

"Yeah!" said Babs. "All taxis should be like this!"

Fizza smiled to herself. Billy and Babs were behaving like two excited children going for a pony ride.

Eventually, Fletcher turned the carriage into a quiet road with large, expensive houses on each side. They looked at all the houses until they saw one with a large gold "S" on the iron gate.

"That's Scully's house!" said Babs. "I recognize his cars!"

Sure enough, there were several expensive cars parked in the driveway. Billy whistled.

"Nice," he said.

Fletcher stopped the carriage across the street, where they were hidden by a large tree.

"Look!" he said.

The gates to Scully's house were open and they could see a white van. It was the van that had taken Golden away.

"Come on, Fletcher!" whispered Fizza. "Let's get your horse back!"

She jumped down from the carriage and ran across the road. Fletcher followed her. They saw two men climb down from the van and disappear around the back of Scully's house. The gates were still open, so Fizza and Fletcher ran quietly into the driveway and went to where the van was.

"Golden!" whispered Fletcher. "Are you in there?"

They heard a loud kick from inside the van.

"He's in there," smiled Fizza.

Fletcher started to pull on the back door.

"It's OK, boy, I'll get you out," he said.

At that moment the gates began to close. They were going to be locked inside! Then they heard an ugly little laugh.

"Did you lose something, kids?"

Fizza and Fletcher turned around to see Robert Scully standing at his front door.

"Now, let me see," he said. "One: you're on my land. Two: you're stealing my van. I think you're breaking the law, don't you? Should we see what the police think? I'll give them a call, should I?"

He pulled his cell phone from his top pocket. At this moment, they heard another laugh. This time it was Billy. He had his face pressed against the gate.

"I wouldn't worry about that, Mr. Scully!" he shouted. "They're already here!"

Fizza, Fletcher, and Scully listened. They heard the unmistakable sound of a police car. As soon as it stopped, the back door opened and Richard McIntyre got out. He was holding a CD of the video of Scully's truck dropping garbage on Park Hill.

What a night it had been! And the next few days were even more extraordinary. Robert Scully lost his business because, with the help of the video, the police discovered that he was responsible for all of the garbage left in green areas in Birmingham. Fizza and Fletcher (and Billy and Babs) were in all the newspapers. There were pictures of the Bullring Kid and the Country Cowboy everywhere.

The Richard McIntyre Horse and Carriage Company became a huge success. People wanted to use the carriages for all sorts of reasons, which included getting to work, going out to dinner, and getting married! The number of passengers grew and extra horses and carriages were brought in to help. Birmingham was very, very proud of its new, "green" taxi service.

*　*　*

Then one day Richard McIntyre invited Fizza and her parents to his house for Sunday lunch. He cooked a special meal. He had borrowed the recipe from Fizza's mom.

"That was delicious, Richard!" said Rubel.

"Mmm!" said Imran.

"And what did *you* think of my fish curry, Fizza?" asked Richard.

"It was nicer than … Robert Scully!" she said.

And they all laughed because everything was nicer than Robert Scully. Then Richard was suddenly serious.

"Listen, kids. I have some news for you."

He paused. Fletcher and Fizza looked at him. They both knew something was wrong.

"I've decided to return to Sark," he said.

"But why, Dad?" said Fletcher.

"Birmingham's not for me, son."

"But you can't!" said Fizza. "The business is such a success!"

"Well, here's another surprise!" said her dad. "Richard has asked us if we would like to run his business in Birmingham."

"While he goes back to take care of the one on Sark!" added her mom.

"So there will be a Birmingham McIntyre Horse and Carriage Company ..." laughed Imran.

"And a Sark one!" said Richard.

"And if the business does well, we're even hoping to buy Scully's land!" said her mom.

Fizza couldn't believe what she was hearing. This was exciting news and terrible news all at the same time!

"And listen to this, Fletcher," said Richard. "You don't have to go. You can stay with Rubel, Imran, and Fizza."

Fletcher paused. He looked at Fizza and then at his dad.

"It's OK, Dad," he said quietly. "I'll come home with you."

He smiled at Fizza. She smiled back, but she couldn't stop the tears running down her face.

* * *

And so, once again Fizza stood beside Richard McIntyre as he arranged the luggage. This time he wasn't loading them onto a boat, he was loading them onto a horse trailer; and it wasn't her luggage, it was Fletcher's. As she helped them put their bags in, she remembered what she'd been like at the beginning of the summer vacation – shy, quiet, maybe even a little dull? Fletcher McIntyre had changed her! He'd made her who she was now! OK, Billy and Babs were good friends, but Fletcher was so much more than that.

She was too shy to tell him, but she didn't want him to go.

"Fizza?"

She turned to see Fletcher standing behind her.

"Well, we're ready to go," he said.

"Great!" she lied, smiling.

Fletcher looked at her. He wasn't going to miss Birmingham but, the truth was, he didn't want to leave Fizza. This girl had changed him. She had stopped him being angry, bad-tempered, and rude. She had taught him how to have fun and how to make friends!

But now she looked happy! Maybe she didn't care that he was going! After all, he thought, she has Billy!

They stood facing one another without speaking. She

could see a boy who had wide green eyes and little brown freckles on his nose, and he could see a girl with warm, kind eyes and thick, black hair that curled around her pretty face. They spoke at exactly the same moment.

"I don't want to go, you know," he said.

"I don't want you to go, you know," she said.

And then they laughed.

"But I have to go with Dad – he doesn't have anyone else."

"I understand. I'd do the same."

"And try not to get into any more trouble – at least not without me, that is."

"What do you mean?"

"Well, if there's any trouble in Birmingham, I should be there."

Fizza smiled. Suddenly she felt a lot happier. "And if there's any trouble in Sark, I should be there!" she said.

"See you around, Bullring Kid."

"See you, Country Cowboy."

Fletcher McIntyre climbed into the horse trailer beside his dad and, within seconds, they had completely disappeared from view.

LOOKING BACK

● ●

1 Check your answers to *Looking forward* on page 65.

ACTIVITIES

● ●

2 Complete the sentences with the names in the box.

Billy   Scully (x3)   Babs (x2)   Fizza   Fletcher

1 .... *Scully* .... wants the land where the stables are.
2 .... is scared of a dog.
3 .... is taken shopping by some new friends.
4 .... apologizes for not being nice.
5 .... interviews someone.
6 .... has the name of a dog as a password.
7 .... destroys a cell phone.
8 .... sends an e-mail from a cell phone.

3 Put the sentences in order.
1 Fizza discovers Scully's password. ☐
2 Fletcher phones Fizza. ☐
3 Babs phones Fizza. ☐
4 Fletcher and Billy manage to escape from the factory. ☐
5 The police go to Scully's factory. ☐
6 Babs goes to interview Scully. ☐ *1*
7 Fizza gets into Scully's e-mail account. ☐
8 Fizza finds an interesting e-mail. ☐

4 **Match the two parts of the sentences.**

1 Scully's drivers make lots of noise with their trucks [_h_]
2 Billy's father lost his job with Scully before ☐
3 When Fizza reads Scully's e-mails, she discovers that ☐
4 When Fizza and Fletcher go to Park Hill, they see ☐
5 Scully puts Fizza's mom's phone in the mug of tea because ☐
6 Scully says Golden may disappear if ☐
7 They manage to get the horse and carriage out because ☐
8 Scully loses his business after the police see ☐

a anyone calls the police.
b he could find out any secrets.
c Billy moves the truck.
d he had told his drivers to get rid of garbage in Park Hill.
e he wants to destroy Fizza's video.
f Scully's men getting rid of garbage there.
g the video Fizza made.
h̶ to scare the horses.

5 **Answer the questions.**

1 How does Fletcher help Billy with the black dog?

....

2 How does Fizza feel about Fletcher becoming more popular?

....

3 What does Babs think of Scully's wife?

....

4 How do Fizza and Fletcher get back to the stable from Park Hill?

....

5 What's going to happen to Richard's green taxi service in Birmingham?

....

6 How does Fizza feel about Fletcher leaving Birmingham?

....

Glossary

[1]**holiday** (page 7) *noun*　British English for 'vacation'

[2]**greedily** (page 7) *adverb*　(here) behaving in a way where you take more food than you need

[3]**pollution** (page 7) *noun*　when air, water or air is dirty with chemicals or waste

[4]**Council** (page 7) *noun*　the group of people elected to govern a town or city and organize services for it

[5]**sigh** (page 8) *verb*　to breathe out slowly and noisily in order to express a strong feeling; (here) to express irritation

[6]**shop** (page 9) *noun*　British English for 'store'

[7]**glad** (page 15) *adjective*　pleased and happy

[8]**cottage** (page 18) *noun*　a small house, usually in the countryside

[9]**carriage** (page 18) *noun*　a vehicle with four wheels, which is usually pulled by horses

[10]**whistle** (page 31) *noun*　to make a sound by breathing air out through a small hole

[11]**ignore** (page 50) *verb*　to not give attention to someone or something

[12]**flood** (page 50) *verb*　to fill or cover in large amounts

[13]**hero** (page 50) *noun*　a person who is admired for having done something special

[14]**unload** (page 51) *verb*　to remove the contents of something, especially things from a vehicle

[15]**astonishment** (page 60) *noun*　very great surprise

[16]**growl** (page 70) *verb*　a deep, rough sound made in the throat; (here) the sound made by an angry dog

[17]**gather** (page 70) *verb*　to come together in a group

[18]**upset** (page 75) *adjective*　worried, unhappy, or angry

[19]**for goodness' sake** (page 78) *expression*　used to emphasize a point we are making, usually when we are irritated or angry

[20]**rubbish** (page 80) *noun*　British English for 'garbage'